Sound It Out

Short Vowels

by Wiley Blevins
illustrated by Sean O'Neill

BOOKS™

Red Chair Press   Egremont, Massachusetts

Look! Books are produced and published by Red Chair Press:
Red Chair Press LLC   PO Box 333   South Egremont, MA 01258-0333
www.redchairpress.com

 FREE activity page from www.redchairpress.com/free-activities

Wiley Blevins is an early-reading specialist and author of the best-selling *Phonics from A to Z: A Practical Guide* from Scholastic and *A Fresh Look at Phonics* from Corwin. Wiley has taught elementary school in both the United States and in South America. He has written more than 70 books for children and 15 for teachers, as well as created reading programs for schools in the U.S. and Asia.

Publisher's Cataloging-In-Publication Data

Names: Blevins, Wiley. | O'Neill, Sean, 1968- illustrator.

Title: Short vowels / by Wiley Blevins ; illustrated by Sean O'Neill.

Description: Egremont, Massachusetts : Red Chair Press, [2019] | Series: Look! books : Sound it out | Includes word-building examples. | Interest age level: 004-008. | Summary: "The alphabet has 26 letters. Five of them are vowels: a-e-i-o-u. They can make long and short sounds. The short vowels can be used to build many simple words. Readers learn what these short vowels can do."--Provided by publisher.

Identifiers: ISBN 9781634403405 (library hardcover) | ISBN 9781634403528 (paperback) | ISBN 9781634403467 (ebook)

Subjects: LCSH: English language--Vowels--Juvenile literature. | English language--Pronunciation--Juvenile literature. | CYAC: English language--Vowels. | English language--Pronunciation.

Classification: LCC PE1157 .B543 2019 (print) | LCC PE1157 (ebook) | DDC 428.13--dc23

LCCN: 2017963413

Copyright © 2019 Red Chair Press LLC
RED CHAIR PRESS, the RED CHAIR and associated logos are registered trademarks of Red Chair Press LLC.

All rights reserved. No part of this book may be reproduced, stored in an information or retrieval system, or transmitted in any form by any means, electronic, mechanical including photocopying, recording, or otherwise without the prior written permission from the Publisher. For permissions, contact info@redchairpress.com

Illustrations by Sean O'Neill

Photo credits: iStock

Printed in the United States of America

0918 1P CGS19

Vowels can make long sounds.
These long vowels say their names.

A-E-I-O-U

Vowels can make short sounds, too.
Let's see what these **short vowels** can do.

Table of Contents

A 4
E 6
I 8
O 10
U 12
Let's Build Words 14

Short a

Say the word <u>apple</u>. What's the first sound you hear?

It's the <u>Short a</u> sound. Say this sound three times: "a"…"a"…"a".

Bite that apple.

Yum!

Short e

Say the boy's name <u>Ed</u>. What's the first sound you hear?

It's the <u>Short e</u> sound. Say this sound three times: "e"…"e"…"e".

Ed rides the elephant up the hill.

Short i

Look at the picture. That's one big insect!

What's the first sound you hear in <u>insect</u>?

It's the <u>Short i</u> sound. Say this sound three times: "i"…"i"…"i".

That big insect is crawling up your leg. *Ick!*

Short o

Hop. Hop. Hop. The frog sits on top of the rock.

What's the first sound you hear in <u>on</u>?

It's the <u>Short o</u> sound. Say this sound three times: "o"…"o"…"o".

Ribbit!

Hop off the rock frog.

Short u

It's raining outside. What do you need? An umbrella!

What's the first sound you hear in <u>umbrella</u>?

It's the <u>Short u</u> sound. Say this sound three times: "u"…"u"…"u".

Up, up, up goes the umbrella.

Let's Build Words

These are the five short vowel sounds. These short sounds are often found in short words. We can make some of these short words.

How many letters will we use? Only three. What words can we make?

Let's see!

Say the sound for m.
Now say the sound for a.
Put the two together: ma.
Add the sound for t
to the end.
What word did you make?

mat

The fat cat sat on the mat.

Or did it?

Say the sound for p.
Now say the sound for i.
Put the two together: pi.
Add the sound for g
to the end.
What word did you make?

pig

The big pig
has a big wig.

I wonder why?

Say the sound for <u>m</u>.
Now say the sound for <u>o</u>.
Put the two together: <u>mo</u>.
Add the sound for <u>m</u>
to the end.
What word did you make?

mom

Give mom a big hug!

Say the sound for s.
Now say the sound for u.
Put the two together: su.
Add the sound for n
to the end.
What word did you make?

sun

Let's have fun
in the sun.

But bring a fan.
It's hot, hot, hot!

22

Say the sound for <u>r</u>.
Now say the sound for <u>e</u>.
Put the two together: <u>re</u>.
Add the sound for <u>d</u>
to the end.
What word did you make?

red

Red is a tomato, an apple, and my favorite crayon.

What is your favorite color?

Now let's have some more fun with short vowel words.

Say the word pan. Change the first letter to m. Presto! You made a new word.

It's a **man** made of metal.

Go, robot man, go!

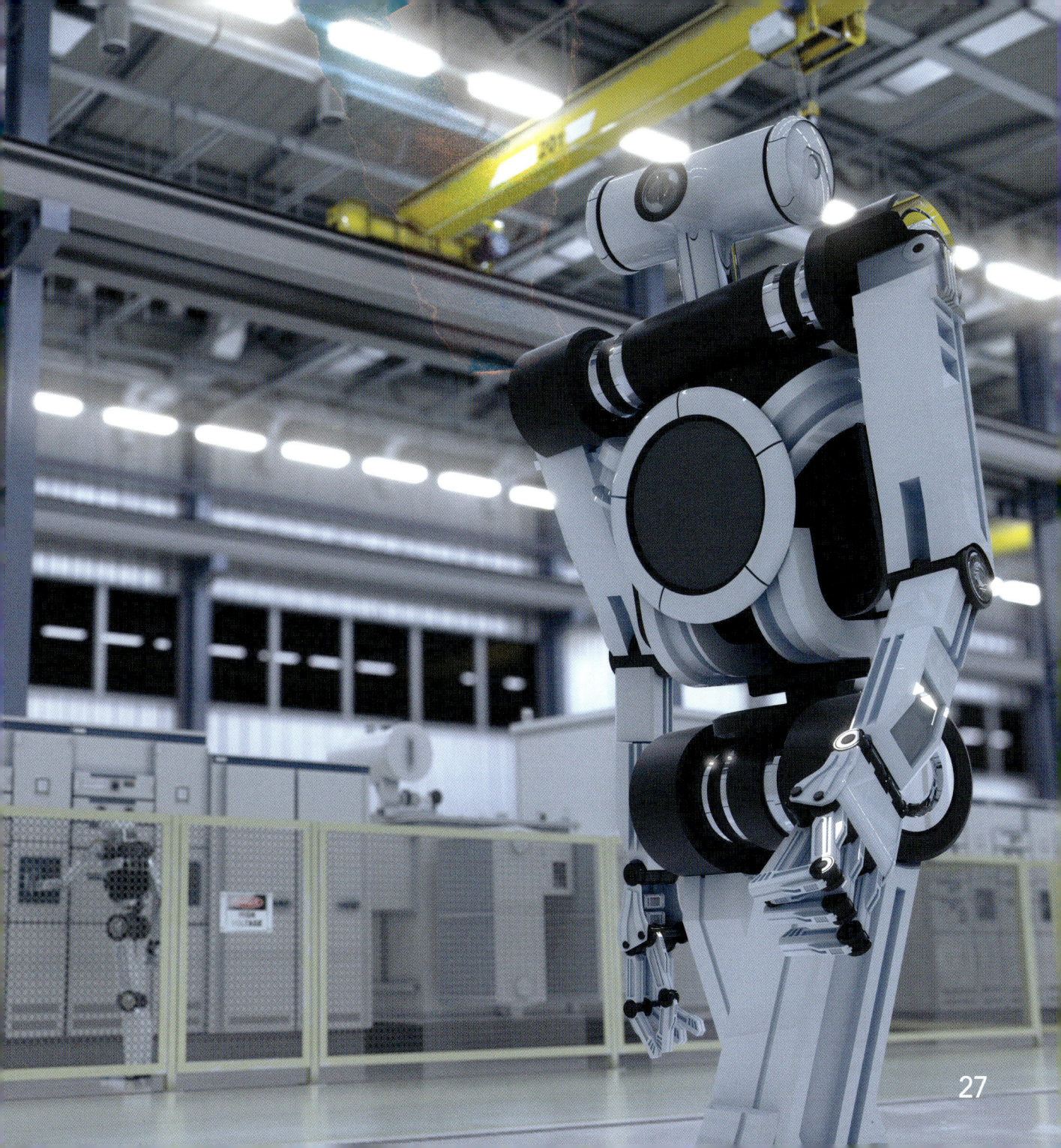

Say the word bat. Change the last letter to g. Presto! You made another new word.

It's **bag**.

Do you think the bat is inside? Go on. Take a look.

A bat in a bag!

Let's try one more.

Say the word fan.
Change the middle letter
to u. Presto! You made **fun**.

Making words
is a lot of fun.

But now it seems
we are all done.

Vowels can make long sounds. These vowels say their names.

A-E-I-O-U

Vowels can make short sounds, too.

Now you know what these **short vowels** can do.